Originally published on May, 2019, in a novel by Cathy McGough as Jump Like a Caribou.
All Rights Reserved. No part of this publication may be reproduced or transmitted in any form or by any means, electronic or mechanical, including photocopy, recording or any other information storage and retrieval system, without prior permission in writing from the publisher.
Published by Stratford Living Publishing
ISBN 978-1-990332-34-0
ISBN Print: 978-1-988201-84-9 (New Version Released 2021)
© Cathy McGough 2011
Cathy McGough has asserted her right under the Copyright, Designs and Patents Act, 1988 to be identified as the author of this work.
This is a work of fiction. The characters in it are all fiction. Resemblance to any persons living or dead is purely coincidental. Names, characters, places and incidents either are the products of the author's imagination or are used fictitiously.

Dedicated to Shannon.

Ever have one of those days?

When you're feeling down and blue?

You'd rather stay in bed...

I'll tell you what to do

Jump Jump Jump

Like a caribou!

Monday's just another day

Too much homework to do!

Then when you can finally play outside -

You can't find your favourite shoes!

Here's what you can do...

Jump Jump Jump

Like a caribou!

Then you'll feel happy

Then you'll be glad

You'll have the very best time

You've ever had!

All you've gotta do

Is Jump Jump Jump

When it's raining outside

Or you're sick with the flu

Scrunch up your hair and

Jump Jump Jump

Like a caribou!

I'll bet you've never seen a sad caribou

Nor a sad calf, have you?

That's because they know

Exactly what to do

Jump Jump Jump

Like a caribou!

Then you'll feel happy

Then you'll be glad

You'll have the very best time

You've ever had!

All you've gotta do

Is Jump Jump Jump

Like a caribou!

JUMP SERIES:
JUMP LIKE A KANGAROO
JUMP AND SAY VALENTINE'S DAY IS FOR KIDS TO
JUMP FOR EVERYTHING BLUE
JUMP AND SAY WHO WHO
JUMP AND SAY P.U.
JUMP AT THE ZOO
JUMP AND SAY BOO
JUMP AND SAY HAPPY BIRTHDAY TO YOU.
OTHER CHILDREN'S BOOKS
BILLIE SHAKESPEARE
BILLY SHAKESPEARE

CPSIA information can be obtained
at www.ICGtesting.com
Printed in the USA
LVHW071949150622
721366LV00020B/627